CHALLENGES FOR DEMOCRACY

The Supreme Court: Activism Versus Restraint

John Allen

ReferencePoint Press

San Diego, CA

About the Author

John Allen is a writer who lives in Oklahoma City.

Picture Credits:
Cover: DNY59/iStock (top left); Joseph Sohm/Shutterstock (top right); Fred Schilling, Collection of the Supreme Court of the United States (bottom)

4: Maury Aaseng
7: Xinhua/Alamy Stock Photo
11: White House Photo/Alamy Stock Photo
14: IanDagnall Computing/Alamy Stock Photo
17: Pictorial Press Ltd/Alamy Stock Photo
21: Bob Daemmrich/Alamy Stock Photo
23: Associated Press
26: Mike Flippo/Shutterstock Images
32: Hanna Kuprevich/Alamy Stock Photo
35: B Christopher/Alamy Stock Photo
41: Jeffrey Isaac Greenberg 18+/Alamy Stock Photo
43: Associated Press
45: WDC Photos/Alamy Stock Photo
50: Travelwide/Alamy Stock Photo
53: World History Archive/Alamy Stock Photo
56: © New York Public Library/Bridgeman Images

LIBRARY OF CONGRESS CATALOGING-IN-PUBLICATION DATA

Names: Allen, John, 1957- author.
Title: The Supreme Court : activism versus restraint / by John Allen.
Description: San Diego, CA : ReferencePoint Press, Inc., 2023. | Series: Challenges for democracy series | Includes bibliographical references and index.
Identifiers: LCCN 2021062748 (print) | LCCN 2021062749 (ebook) | ISBN 9781678203085 (library binding) | ISBN 9781678203092 (ebook)
Subjects: LCSH: United States. Supreme Court--Juvenile literature. | Judicial process--United States--Juvenile literature. | Political questions and judicial power--United States--Juvenile literature.
Classification: LCC KF8742 .A755 2023 (print) | LCC KF8742 (ebook) | DDC 347.73/26--dc23/eng/20220202
LC record available at https://lccn.loc.gov/2021062748
LC ebook record available at https://lccn.loc.gov/2021062749

CONTENTS

American democracy has been experiencing many challenges. Foremost among those challenges is the widespread perception that US democracy is either "in trouble" or "failing." This is the view of a majority of young Americans, age eighteen to twenty-nine. A national poll conducted in Fall 2021 by the Harvard Kennedy School Institute of Politics finds that only 7 percent of young adults view the United States as a "healthy democracy."

Which of the following phrases best describes the United States today?

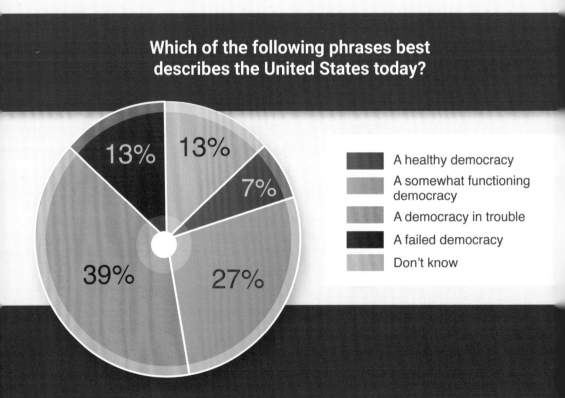

13% | 13% | 7% | 39% | 27%

- A healthy democracy
- A somewhat functioning democracy
- A democracy in trouble
- A failed democracy
- Don't know

Source: "Harvard Youth Poll," Harvard Kennedy School Institute of Politics, December 1, 2021. https://iop.harvard.edu.

Restraint in a Time of Polarization

In October 2020, Notre Dame Law School professor Amy Coney Barrett faced a barrage of questions from Democrats on the Senate Judiciary Committee during her confirmation hearing. Barrett was then-president Donald Trump's choice to replace Supreme Court justice Ruth Bader Ginsburg, who had died one month earlier. Court observers on the political left feared that Barrett's confirmation, tilting the court six to three in favor of conservatives, would usher in a dangerous wave of judicial activism. In essence, they worried that Barrett and the other right-leaning justices would decide cases according to their political preferences instead of by neutral analysis of the law.

One particular concern was the fate of the Affordable Care Act (ACA), a controversial 2010 health care law that had narrowly survived two earlier challenges in the Supreme Court. The ACA is often referred to as *Obamacare* because Republican opponents of Democratic president Barack Obama wanted the public to reject it as a failed project of the then-liberal White House. Barrett, however, insisted that her political views would play no part in her decision on cases regarding the ACA or other partisan issues. "Nobody wants to live in accord with the law of Amy," she told the senators. "I'm sure not even my children would want to do that."[1] The answer affirmed the nonpartisan role many in America expect a justice would adopt, but it did not sway liberals in the

Senate. All forty-seven Democrats voted against Barrett's confirmation. Nonetheless, she was confirmed by a vote of fifty-two to forty-eight.

On June 17, 2021, the court, now including Justice Barrett, handed down its decision in *California v. Texas,* the challenge to the ACA. In a seven-to-two ruling, the court upheld the law. Barrett joined the majority in deciding that the plaintiffs in Texas had failed to establish their standing to sue. Legal experts noted that a coalition of four liberals and three conservatives had opted for judicial restraint, keeping the ACA in place and leaving any sweeping changes in the law up to legislators. "If Obamacare is going to be dramatically changed," said Case Western law professor Jonathan Adler, "that's something that Congress will have to do."[2]

Impartiality Versus Bias on the Court

Justice Barrett's confirmation hearing showed how the Supreme Court reflects the political divisiveness in the United States. Americans, not to mention the justices themselves, often disagree on the court's procedures and its decisions. And even though each justice is sworn to apply the nation's laws impartially, polls show that many people believe the justices too often rule according to their own political biases.

Nonetheless, appointments to the Supreme Court are political in nature. Nominees are chosen by the sitting president and generally share that president's political views. Moreover, justices serve for life unless they decide to step down. A change in the court's political makeup can influence its decisions for years to come. With the stakes of each appointment so high, it is not unusual for senators to grill the other party's nominees in confirmation hearings that can last days. Often nominees are asked how they would rule on a divisive issue, even though they cannot comment on a hypothetical case without opening themselves up to charges of bias. At any rate, politics is never far from discussions of the court's business.

US Supreme Court nominee Amy Coney Barrett answers questions during her confirmation hearing before the Senate Judiciary Committee in October 2020. She was confirmed nine days before the election of a new president.

Judicial Activism Versus Judicial Restraint

Much of the current debate about the Supreme Court's proper role focuses on judicial activism. This is often defined as legislating from the bench, or making up the law rather than simply interpreting it. Justices are accused of judicial activism when they seem to be pursuing a political agenda instead of ruling from a constitutional standpoint. Judicial activism can also mean deciding an issue that otherwise would be left to state or local lawmakers. In its 2015 decision in *Obergefell v. Hodges,* the court ruled that same-sex couples had the right to marry according to the due process and equal protection clauses in the Fourteenth Amendment. Although many Americans hailed the decision as a victory for civil rights, critics argued that the court had engaged in judicial activism by discovering a hitherto unknown constitutional right.

The opposite of judicial activism is judicial restraint. This can mean a reluctance to overrule congressional laws because voters can do this themselves via the ballot box. For example, some observers believe the current court has displayed judicial restraint in upholding the ACA three times. Judicial restraint can also refer to ruling strictly by the letter of the law, or the law's plain language. Justices may even delve into transcripts of congressional debates to find out what the original lawmakers intended.

In today's polarized landscape, one side's judicial activism can be the other side's judicial restraint. Because claims of "activism" and "restraint" depend on the views of the speaker, many legal experts consider the terms to be partisan. As Ilya Shapiro, director of the Robert A. Levy Center for Constitutional Studies, has remarked, "Quite often, 'activist' is synonymous with any decision the speaker doesn't like, and 'restraint' means the judge is being wise."[3] Nevertheless, the political leanings of the justices as well as their past judicial opinions are often highlighted when deeply polarizing issues reach the court. And whatever decision the court hands down, the ruling will likely not be popular with all Americans, inviting critics to infer political bias.

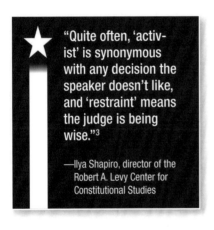

"Quite often, 'activist' is synonymous with any decision the speaker doesn't like, and 'restraint' means the judge is being wise."[3]

—Ilya Shapiro, director of the Robert A. Levy Center for Constitutional Studies

In April 2022 President Joe Biden's first Supreme Court nominee, Judge Ketanji Brown Jackson, was confirmed by a vote of fifty-three to forty-seven. Three Republican senators joined with all fifty Senate Democrats to confirm Jackson, making her the first Black woman to join the court. Jackson's liberal judicial philosophy, influenced by her background as a public defender, contrasts with Barrett's more conservative views. Inevitably, some commentators will interpret Jackson's or Barrett's decisions as conforming to their personal or political bias. No justice seems safe from such accusations. But whether the court's rulings going forward constitute judicial activism or restraint must be left to the American public—and the judgment of history.

CHAPTER ONE

The Supreme Court's Role in a Healthy Democracy

Recent years have seen several bitter political wrangles over the makeup of the Supreme Court. Each side—liberal and conservative—fears the appointment of new justices could tilt the court too far the other way. In February 2016, the death of Justice Antonin Scalia seemed to provide President Barack Obama with an opportunity to shift the court's balance to the left. Scalia was a conservative icon with tremendous influence. His written "dissents" against the majority opinion sometimes criticized the court for engaging in judicial activism. Obama sought to replace Scalia with Merrick Garland, a widely respected federal appeals court judge who was considered a moderate liberal.

With the next presidential election nine months away, Mitch McConnell, the leader of the Republican-controlled Senate, argued that Obama should not appoint a justice so close to the end of his presidential term and that American voters should have a say in the selection of a new justice to replace Scalia. With this in mind, McConnell announced he would not hold hearings for Obama's nominee. McConnell's move outraged Democrats and much of the national media, who saw it as an abuse of his power as Senate majority leader.

In the end McConnell's gambit paid off for Republicans. Donald Trump, the party's candidate for the White House, won the 2016 election. He went on to name Neil Gorsuch, a staunch conservative, to fill the vacancy on the court. The episode showed how politics plays a significant part in determining the high court's makeup.

A Legal Body Free from Political Pressure

Rachel Shelden, associate professor of history at Pennsylvania State University, says the focus on partisanship regarding the Supreme Court is nothing new. "Early Americans would have recognized the kinds of partisan political conversations we are having about the court today," says Shelden, "but they would have been shocked to discover how much power we have given the judiciary over our democracy."[4] The American founders had one main purpose in creating the Supreme Court: to protect the people's rights and liberties from being eroded or taken away by the government. The means of protecting these rights was to enforce the Constitution's limits on government power. To check the powers wielded by the executive and legislative branches of government, the Supreme Court acts as the final authority on what the Constitution means.

Details of the Supreme Court's makeup and operation are not spelled out in the Constitution. It merely states that "the judicial Power of the United States, shall be vested in one supreme Court, and in such inferior Courts as the Congress may from time to time ordain and establish."[5] In 1789, as one of its first acts, Congress set up the federal court system. It consisted of three levels: trial courts, appeals courts, and the Supreme Court. The first Supreme Court had six justices, but in 1869 Congress increased the total to nine. The odd number has proved essential in deciding cases where the justices are narrowly split.

The founders also sought to make the Supreme Court a legal body free from political pressure. It left confirmation of the president's nominees for the court to the Senate, instead of the more

Merrick Garland accepts President Barack Obama's nomination to the US Supreme Court in March 2016. Citing the presidential election still eight months away, Senate majority leader Mitch McConnell blocked the Senate from even considering Obama's nominee.

rancorous House of Representatives. Most important, the Supreme Court was made one of three coequal branches of the US government. The court's decisions have the power of law, even when they overrule acts by the other two branches. This supports the founders' idea of checks and balances in the federal government. The power of each branch is subject to limitations from the other branches. For example, the Supreme Court generally cannot initiate cases on its own. Cases must come from a lower court. Only in special circumstances does the Supreme Court have original jurisdiction to hear a case. These include a dispute between states or a matter concerning ambassadors or public ministers.

Marbury v. Madison and Judicial Review

Since the Supreme Court's role was not clearly defined in the Constitution, its authority had to be established by other means. John Marshall, the court's fourth chief justice, deserves credit

The Influence of Law Clerks

A major power of the Supreme Court is its ability to choose the cases it hears. But the justices themselves can be influenced in their choices by a source that is sometimes overlooked: their law clerks. Every year, thirty-six young lawyers are picked for these coveted positions. They come from the nation's top law schools and usually have served with distinction under a federal appeals court judge. Each Supreme Court justice employs four law clerks to help with administrative duties and conduct legal research. Law clerks also prepare briefs on the cases submitted for certiorari, reviewing the key issues raised and the rulings of lower courts. By emphasizing certain points and downplaying others, the clerks can help sway a justice on whether or not the court should hear a case. Moreover, they frequently influence the court's final rulings—especially in high-profile cases.

Some experts have warned that law clerks, while excellent students of the law, are growing increasingly partisan. "We are getting a composition of the clerk work force that is getting to be like the House of Representatives," said David J. Garrow, a historian of the court. "Each side is putting forward only ideological purists."

Quoted in Adam Liptak, "A Sign of the Court's Polarization: Choice of Clerks," *New York Times*, September 6, 2010. www.nytimes.com.

for expanding and affirming the court's powers. This includes its most important power: judicial review, which is ruling on whether laws and acts of government are constitutional.

The Marshall court's action stemmed from *Marbury v. Madison,* a complicated minor case about a political appointment. In 1801, new president Thomas Jefferson had his secretary of state, James Madison, prevent William Marbury from being seated as justice of the peace in the District of Columbia. Marbury, a member of the Federalist Party like the previous president, John Adams, was one of many judges and officials Adams appointed at the end of his term to preserve his party's power. On February 24, 1803, the Marshall court ruled by a vote of six to zero that it did not have jurisdiction in the case and could not force Madison to seat Marbury. The court decided that the relevant section of the Judiciary Act of 1789 was unconstitutional because it gave the Supreme Court too much power over the executive branch. In effect, by acknowledging limits on the court's reach in this particular case, Marshall vastly expanded its power to rule on whether congressional laws conflict with the Constitution. The principle of judicial review gives the Supreme Court an active role in ensuring that Congress and the executive branch act within constitutional bounds. "The powers of the Legislature are defined and limited," Marshall wrote in his *Marbury* opinion, "and [so] that those limits may not be mistaken or forgotten, the constitution is written."[6]

Judicial Review and the Civil Rights Movement

Despite the *Marbury* ruling, the Supreme Court showed reluctance to overrule Congress. Several decades would pass before the court again declared a congressional act unconstitutional. In 1857, the court ruled against Congress's antislavery Missouri Compromise in *Dred Scott v. Sanford*. The law had entitled escaped slaves such as Scott to live in freedom in nonslaveholding states. Instead, the Supreme Court ruled that people of African descent, whether free or enslaved, were not legally American citizens and could not sue in federal court. In addition, the court allowed slave owners to pursue escaped Blacks into free territory. The *Dred Scott* decision demonstrated that judicial review did not necessarily lead to social justice. The ruling, widely reviled in the North and among opponents of slavery, was a factor that led eventually to the Civil War.

In the 1896 case *Plessy v. Ferguson,* the court refused to employ judicial review to uphold the rights of Black Americans. In *Plessy,* it ruled that racial segregation under the policy of "separate but equal" was constitutional. This legalized so-called Jim Crow laws in the South that permitted separate public accommodations for Blacks in everything from restaurants and hotels to drinking fountains. Justice John Marshall Harlan, the lone dissenter in the seven-to-one decision, predicted that *Plessy* would rank with *Dred Scott* as a disastrous mistake. "Our Constitution

In 1896 the Supreme Court ruled that racial segregation under the guise of "separate but equal" was constitutional. Segregated facilities, such as this bus station waiting area in 1940s North Carolina, continued to be the norm in much of the South.

is color-blind," wrote Harlan, "and neither knows nor tolerates classes among citizens."[7]

During the twentieth century, the court began to employ judicial review more frequently. And unlike the decisions in *Dred Scott* and *Plessy,* its rulings often served to uphold and expand civil rights. Fifty-eight years after the *Plessy* case, the Supreme Court struck down the practice of segregation. In *Brown v. Board of Education of Topeka*, the court unanimously held that separate facilities are by their very nature unequal and infringed on Black Americans' civil rights. Two of the justices hesitated, suggesting that such a crucial decision belonged in Congress, but finally they were convinced to join the majority. The court's 1954 *Brown* ruling wiped out state laws mandating segregated schools as violations of the equal protection clause of the Fourteenth

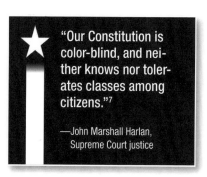

"Our Constitution is color-blind, and neither knows nor tolerates classes among citizens."[7]

—John Marshall Harlan, Supreme Court justice

Amendment. The Constitution had not changed, but American society had, with rising demands for racial justice. And it seems the court was swayed by the temper of the times. According to Michael J. Nelson, associate professor of political science at Pennsylvania State University, "Most of the evidence suggests that the court's decisions particularly on important issues tend to be congruent with public opinion."[8]

The Ability to Choose Cases Under Appeal

Along with judicial review, another important power of the Supreme Court is its ability to choose its cases. This power derives from the court's authority to hear appeals from lower courts. With rare exceptions, the justices can decide whether or not to hear a case. This enables the Supreme Court to resolve conflicts between lower court rulings. It may also want to reaffirm a past decision that one of the circuit courts has seemingly ignored. Choosing cases provides the court an opportunity to rule on the

How Congress Can Respond to Supreme Court Rulings

Judicial review enables the Supreme Court to declare a congressional act void because it violates the Constitution. This is known as a constitutional ruling, and it can only be overridden by the difficult process of passing an amendment to the Constitution. However, the court also issues what are called statutory rulings that seek to clarify ambiguity in the way specific laws are written. In such a case, Congress can act to lessen the impact of the court's decision by rewriting the statute or by passing a new law.

One example is a case involving equal rights in the workplace. After retiring from her job as supervisor at a Goodyear tire plant in Alabama in 1998, Lilly Ledbetter had sued the company for not giving her pay raises comparable to male employees in the same position. The Supreme Court ruled that Title VII of the Civil Rights Act, guaranteeing equal treatment in the workplace, set a 180-day limit for filing for back pay, which Ledbetter had failed to meet. To counter future bad outcomes following the court's decision, Congress passed the 2009 Lilly Ledbetter Fair Pay Act. The law makes it easier to recover back wages owed due to discrimination.

most contentious issues of the day—or to avoid them if it prefers leaving those cases to legislators.

The Supreme Court's power to handpick cases was codified in the Judiciary Act of 1925, also known as the Certiorari Act. (*Certiorari* is Latin for "to be more fully informed.") In asking the court to review its case, a party submits a petition called a writ of certiorari. The court receives more than seven thousand petitions each year, including records from the lower court's proceedings. Law clerks for each justice review the materials and write memos that summarize the issues and advise on whether a case is worth hearing. The cases that make the cut often address an important legal question or social issue. From among the petitions, the Supreme Court agrees to hear only about eighty to one hundred cases per year. Cases are chosen following a period of discussion and a formal vote by the justices. If four of the nine justices vote to hear a case, the court grants the petition of certiorari.

A Lack of Enforcement Power

The Supreme Court may be able to select its cases, but it does not have the power to enforce its rulings. It depends on the executive and legislative branches for enforcement. Although the court is recognized as the legitimate final authority on federal law and the Constitution, on occasion, its decisions have not been carried out, especially when they are directed at the government. "To give effect to their decisions and orders, courts depend on popular legitimacy and the cooperation of the other branches," Ilya Shapiro has written. "While that cooperation is normally forthcoming when needed to enforce judicial decisions against private citizens, when the subject of a court's order is the government itself, there's always a risk it will be ignored or avoided."[9]

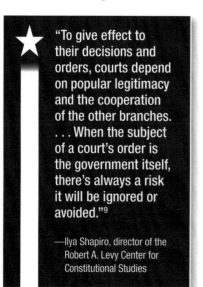

"To give effect to their decisions and orders, courts depend on popular legitimacy and the cooperation of the other branches. . . . When the subject of a court's order is the government itself, there's always a risk it will be ignored or avoided."[9]

—Ilya Shapiro, director of the Robert A. Levy Center for Constitutional Studies

US soldiers escort Black students as they enter the previously all-White Central High School in Little Rock, Arkansas, in 1957. Despite a 1954 Supreme Court ruling outlawing segregation, many school districts continued to maintain segregated schools.

A famous example occurred in 1832 in the case *Worcester v. Georgia*. The state of Georgia sought to apply its laws to lands belonging by treaty to the Cherokee Nation. The Supreme Court, led by Chief Justice Marshall, ruled that Georgia had no authority over the lands. However, President Andrew Jackson opposed the court's decision. Jackson, who wanted Native Americans removed from lands in the Southeast, refused to abide by the ruling. Under his administration, the Cherokee were forcibly moved westward along the infamous Trail of Tears.

The lack of enforcement powers could have stymied *Brown* and other landmark Supreme Court rulings on civil rights. Although the court clearly outlawed segregation in its *Brown* decision, many school districts continued to maintain separate schools for Black children. On September 23, 1957, three years after *Brown,* President Dwight D. Eisenhower sent one thousand US Army troops to Little Rock, Arkansas. The troops surrounded Central High School to guarantee the safety of nine Black students as they entered the otherwise all-White school.

The Supreme Court's *Brown* ruling finally was enforced by the executive branch, acting under the president's authority.

Authority Based on Public Trust

The Supreme Court serves as the final arbiter on the Constitution's meaning. As such, it protects people's rights by enforcing constitutional limits on government power. Its own power rests in interpreting law and recognizing when judicial decisions from the lower courts exceed or contradict the Constitution or other federal statutes. Before being seated on the court, a justice swears to "faithfully and impartially discharge and perform all the duties incumbent upon me."[10] Thus, a justice's duty is to defend the laws of the land and not to advance political agendas.

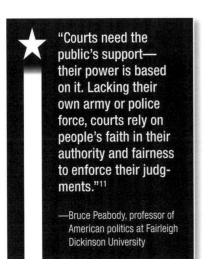

"Courts need the public's support—their power is based on it. Lacking their own army or police force, courts rely on people's faith in their authority and fairness to enforce their judgments."[11]

—Bruce Peabody, professor of American politics at Fairleigh Dickinson University

To a large degree, the Supreme Court's authority rests on the public's trust that it will remain nonpartisan. "Courts need the public's support—their power is based on it," says Bruce Peabody, professor of American politics at Fairleigh Dickinson University. "Lacking their own army or police force, courts rely on people's faith in their authority and fairness to enforce their judgments."[11] To maintain this faith, the court must act fairly and ensure that the rights of citizens are not violated. This is not to say that the justices do not have points of view that may reflect their political leanings. For this reason, some observers believe balancing the political views of the sitting justices is vital to maintaining a Supreme Court that can earn a larger share of the public trust. There is no requirement, though, that the court have an even distribution of conservative and liberal judges. So an imbalance can lead to instances in which public opinion calls into question the evenhandedness of the court's decisions.

CHAPTER TWO

Activism Versus Restraint over the Years

On March 2, 1963, a young woman in Phoenix, Arizona, was kidnapped and raped as she was walking home from work. Shortly afterward, the woman picked Ernesto Miranda out of a police lineup as the man who had abducted her. Miranda immediately was arrested, taken to a separate room, and questioned about the crime. After two hours of interrogation, he wrote out a confession to the crimes and signed it. The paper stated that he had provided the information voluntarily and that he fully understood his rights. However, the paper did not list any specific rights.

Based mainly on the written confession, an Arizona court found Miranda guilty and sentenced him to prison. His attorney, however, appealed the case. He claimed that the confession was invalid because Miranda had not been advised of his right to an attorney or warned that his statements could be used against him. Miranda's appeal eventually reached the Supreme Court. On June 13, 1966, the court ruled five to four that Miranda's written confession was inadmissible because he had not been informed of his right to counsel and his Fifth Amendment right against self-incrimination.

Miranda v. Arizona, with Chief Justice Earl Warren writing for the majority, was widely criticized as an example of reckless judicial activism. Justice Byron White argued in his dissent to the ruling that the Fifth Amendment says nothing about warnings that must be obeyed during police interrogations. Other opponents claimed that police investigations would stall and criminals would go free if such rules were put in place. Nonetheless, delivering so-called Miranda warnings became standard procedure for law officers across the nation. Some jurists, such as White, believed that the court had, in effect, created a new law. "In *Miranda,* the Supreme Court created and imposed a new procedure for interrogating suspects in custody, introducing the famous 'right to remain silent' speech," said Orin S. Kerr, professor at the University of California, Berkeley, School of Law. "The court's decision expanded the lawmaking power of the courts at the expense of the lawmaking power of the other branches of government."[12]

Judicial Activism and the Push for Civil Rights

In its *Miranda* decision, the Warren court affirmed what it believed were the inherent civil rights of all criminal defendants. Prior to the case, interrogation rules had mostly been left up to local law enforcement and state oversight. But Warren stressed that citizens such as Miranda faced a grievous imbalance of power when in police custody. Miranda, a Mexican American of limited means, had been plunged into a hostile atmosphere and subjected to harsh questioning. The court noted similar conditions in three cases combined under the *Miranda* umbrella. Another defendant was an indigent young Black man who had dropped out of school in Los Angeles in the sixth grade. As legal analyst Jay Willis states, "Expecting these men to challenge armed authority figures would treat hundreds of years of racial discrimination and police abuse as if they did not exist."[13]

Judicial activism is based on the idea that judges may shape their rulings in order to obtain a desired result instead of strictly following the law as written. It usually is linked to activism for civil rights and social justice. The first use of the term appeared in a 1947 article by Arthur M. Schlesinger Jr. in *Fortune* magazine.

A Texas police officer reads a handcuffed suspect his Miranda rights. In its 1966 Miranda decision, the Supreme Court affirmed what it believed were the inherent civil rights of all criminal defendants.

Schlesinger, who later served as an adviser to President John F. Kennedy, believed that judicial activists on the bench do not separate law and politics. They assume that it is proper to pursue certain political outcomes when the law, as written, does not produce social justice. According to the judicial activists, explained Schlesinger, "the Court cannot escape politics: therefore, let it use its political power for wholesome social purposes."[14] Instead of painting judicial activism as good or bad, Schlesinger merely described it and noted that it was gaining acceptance.

After Schlesinger's *Fortune* article, most references to judicial activism tended to be negative. Critics often called it legislating from the bench. They condemned the practice as antidemocratic, claiming that it usurped the power of elected lawmakers. And few judges spoke in favor of legislating from the bench. As US District Court judge Louis Pollak once observed, "It seems safe to say that most

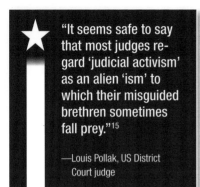

judges regard 'judicial activism' as an alien 'ism' to which their misguided brethren sometimes fall prey."[15] Some commentators pointed out that, even though the term was new, judicial activism had existed for decades. For example, in the early 1900s, the Supreme Court supported the progressive trust-busting movement by ordering the breakup of large-scale monopolies in railroads, oil, sugar, and tobacco. During the Great Depression of the 1930s, the court, after initial opposition, ruled in favor of New Deal programs that granted the federal government sweeping new powers.

Certain justices have earned a reputation as activists. Louis Brandeis, who served on the Supreme Court from 1916 to 1939, believed that the court should influence government policy making with its rulings. In his opinions, Brandeis often explained why a law was not only constitutional but also in the public's best interest. Hugo L. Black, serving from 1937 to 1971, often shaped his opinions to improve social welfare. In 1963, he delivered the lead opinion in *Gideon v. Wainwright,* which established the right to a state-appointed attorney for poor defendants. William J. Brennan Jr., whose term on the court lasted from 1956 to 1990, showed keen awareness of how landmark rulings could affect people's daily lives. In 1962, his majority opinion in *Baker v. Carr* affirmed the court's duty to decide political questions when voting rights come under threat.

The Benefits and Drawbacks of Judicial Activism

Supporters of judicial activism believe it offers major benefits for society. First, it can set up checks and balances against the actions of the other two branches of government. Second, judicial activism can settle constitutional gray areas, where there is no general agreement on the document's meaning. In such cases, the court can use its discretion to create what it considers a practical outcome. Third, it can help deliver a solution when a dispute threatens to drag on too long. For example, in 2000 the Supreme Court intervened in *Bush v. Gore* to end presidential vote recounts in Florida, essentially handing the election to George W. Bush. Many disagreed with the decision, but amid all the turmoil, the court's authority prevailed in the matter. Fourth, judicial activism may be necessary to institute social reforms or protect individual rights when the other two branches fail to act.

At the same time, judicial activism has its drawbacks. As noted, it can lay claim to powers that rightly belong to Congress. Voters may lose faith in the legal system when unelected judges decide questions that are better left to the ballot box. Judicial activists also may be viewed as political actors instead of interpreters of the law. Seeking a certain political outcome instead of ruling

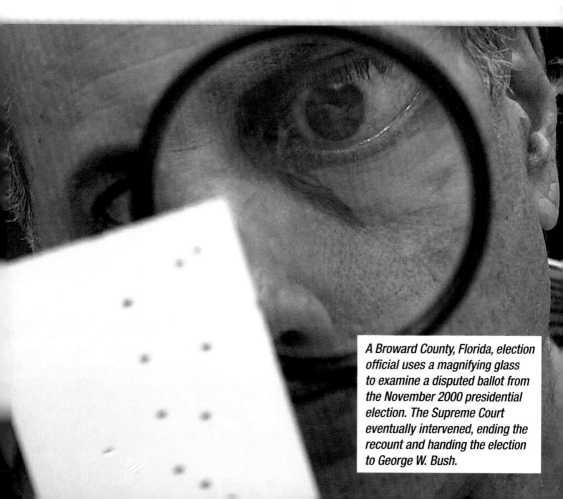

A Broward County, Florida, election official uses a magnifying glass to examine a disputed ballot from the November 2000 presidential election. The Supreme Court eventually intervened, ending the recount and handing the election to George W. Bush.

on the law as written opens the Supreme Court and lower courts to charges of bias and erodes public trust. And when the court is swayed by purely political arguments, it can lead to a sort of mob justice, through which the public's wishes outweigh legal analysis. Such rulings may also create confusion as to what the law is and how it will be enforced.

The Pursuit of Judicial Restraint

Many judges reject judicial activism and pursue its opposite: judicial restraint. These judges strive to follow the law as written instead of introducing their own political preferences. Judges exercise judicial restraint when they hesitate to strike down laws that do not violate the Constitution. They prefer to leave such changes to the legislature and the people's vote.

The US legal system tends to promote judicial restraint. Article III of the Constitution limits so-called standing, or access to federal courts, unless a party can demonstrate an actual injury caused by a defendant. Federal courts do not hear cases just to settle grievances or provide guidance on abstract legal questions. Also, if judges can decide a case on grounds other than a sticky constitutional issue, they do so. Between two readings of a law, they tend to choose the one that avoids questions about the law's constitutional basis. In other words, jurists from federal courts all the way up to the Supreme Court try to avoid barging into constitutional issues if it is not necessary.

Supreme Court justices known for judicial restraint often base their rulings on close readings of the Constitution or the text of a law. They claim to resist political influence on their rulings. They may also hesitate to overturn precedent—an established reading from a prior case—unless there is overwhelming cause. One of the Supreme Court's most famous advocates of judicial restraint was Oliver Wendell Holmes Jr. Appointed by President Theodore Roosevelt in 1902, Holmes served until 1932. Holmes had no problem upholding laws with which he disagreed, even deplored. In his view, it was up to voters and

Practicing Judicial Activism via Restraint During the New Deal

Sometimes the Supreme Court can lean toward social justice goals while seeming to practice judicial restraint. Justice Louis Brandeis is often characterized as a judicial activist. He was appointed in 1916 by President Woodrow Wilson, one of the most progressive presidents in US history. And Brandeis certainly shared Wilson's progressive philosophy. In the early 1930s, Brandeis warned President Franklin D. Roosevelt that his progressive New Deal programs faced strong opposition in the Supreme Court. He advised Roosevelt that his programs needed to be scaled back to gain the court's approval. In May 1935, Brandeis himself joined a unanimous court in striking down three parts of Roosevelt's first New Deal package.

As Roosevelt attacked the court and public sentiment got behind the New Deal, Brandeis's fellow justices reconsidered their stance. When Congress passed more-focused New Deal laws, the Supreme Court, under the influence of Brandeis, withdrew its constitutional objections. By practicing judicial restraint, and allowing the legislature to have its way, the court furthered activist goals.

legislators to change bad laws. "If my fellow citizens want to go to Hell I will help them," he once said. "It's my job."[16] Justice Scalia, whose term extended from 1986 until his death in 2016, was known for his sharply worded views in favor of judicial restraint. In *District of Columbia v. Heller* in 2008, Scalia's majority opinion held that lawmakers could not restrict the Second Amendment right to keep and bear arms.

Stand by the Law and Legal Precedent

Various ideas and legal philosophies are associated with judicial restraint. One of the most important ideas is stare decisis, a Latin term that means "stand by what has been decided." When judges employ stare decisis, they rely on precedents, or previously decided cases. Such cases provide a bedrock of settled law that, according to judicial restraint, should be a strong influence on subsequent courts. Critics charge that stare decisis too often delays social change. The doctrine is certainly not infallible, and past decisions may need to be corrected. But overall, say its supporters, it tends to produce stable results and a healthy sense of continuity in the legal system.

Other approaches focus on the written language of laws and the Constitution. Judges who use the plain meaning rule seek to interpret laws according to the plain, commonsense meaning of their words. In this way, they rule out politically motivated or academic readings that might introduce a modern bias in conflict with the law's plain meaning. An approach related to the plain meaning rule is textualism. This means interpreting the text of a law without resorting to its history or the legislature's intent in passing it. It seeks the obvious meaning that the words convey. Strict constructionism, by contrast, does consider the intent of the lawmakers who passed a statute. However, it focuses strictly on the meaning of the language at the time of the law's passage.

Supreme Court justices known for judicial restraint often base their rulings on close readings of the Constitution. They claim to resist political influence on their rulings.

Heller and Textualism

One of the avenues for judicial restraint is textualism, or relying on close readings of the Constitution's words. The Supreme Court's ruling in *District of Columbia v. Heller* found constitutional support for gun ownership rights in the text of the Second Amendment. The amendment reads, "A well regulated Militia, being necessary to the security of a free State, the right of the people to keep and bear Arms shall not be infringed."

Justice Antonin Scalia argued in his majority opinion that the amendment clearly prohibits the government from infringing on "the right of the people to keep and bear Arms"—that is, to own and use firearms for protection. Yet in this case, textualism also presented pitfalls. In his dissent, Justice John Paul Stevens said that Scalia treated the opening clause of the amendment as if it were just pointless verbiage. To Stevens, the clause has an obvious purpose, linking gun rights to an organized militia. Scalia himself admitted that gun ownership rights had certain limits, such as with felons and the mentally ill. As Richard A. Epstein of the public policy think tank the Hoover Institution notes, "Constitutional interpretation remains so difficult because, though we must start with a scrupulous reading of the text, the law presents innumerable cases that require judges to go beyond it."

Richard A. Epstein, "The Limits of Textualism," *Defining Ideas*, March 5, 2018. www.hoover.org.

Opponents of the plain meaning rule and other text-related rules for judicial restraint point out that word meanings and usage can change radically over decades and centuries. Interpretation is often unavoidable. As Justice Brennan, a staunch judicial activist, said in a 1985 speech,

> We current Justices read the Constitution in the only way that we can: as Twentieth Century Americans. We look to the history of the time of framing and to the intervening history of interpretation. But the ultimate question must be, what do the words of the text mean in our time? For the genius of the Constitution rests not in any static meaning it might have had in a world that is dead and gone, but in the adaptability of its great principles to cope with current problems and current needs.[17]

Judicial Activism and Public Trust

Judges are often labeled as judicial activists when they leave aside the law as written to seek a certain political outcome. Thus, it is not uncommon for opponents of a judicial ruling to view it as politically motivated. The labels of judicial activism or restraint often depend on how judges rule on controversial issues. However, polls show that Americans trust the Supreme Court more when they see it as being above politics. Whether it is the court's responsibility to remain above politics is a question that each justice must decide and a question that American society must face when reexamining the role and purpose of the court.

CHAPTER THREE

The Abortion Controversy

On September 1, 2021, a controversial abortion law went into effect in Texas. The law forbids aborting any pregnancy in which a heartbeat can be detected. Since a fetal heartbeat typically is present at six weeks of pregnancy, the law effectively bans all abortions after six weeks. But the heartbeat requirement is only part of this novel statute. The law also permits people to sue abortion providers or anyone who facilitates an abortion after the six-week period. In this way, it seeks to punish abortion providers not with criminal law enforcement, which would make it subject to judicial review, but through private civil lawsuits.

Since the Supreme Court legalized abortion in *Roe v. Wade* in 1973, pro-life advocates have worked to get the decision overturned. At the same time, they have pushed to get laws passed in several states that place various restrictions on abortion. However, abortion remains a protected right under the Fourteenth Amendment, which courts commonly interpret as guaranteeing personal privacy. Thus, say pro-choice opponents, the Texas law is plainly unconstitutional, even while it seeks to prevent the use of judicial review that would declare it so. In temporarily blocking the so-called Heartbeat Act, district judge Robert Pitman blasted what he saw as its devious attempt to get around the Constitution. "Rather than subjecting its law to judicial review under the Constitution, the State deliberately circumvented the traditional process," wrote Pitman. "It drafted the law with the intent to preclude review by federal courts that have the obligation to safeguard the very rights the statute likely violates."[18]

A Prime Example of Judicial Activism

The Texas Heartbeat Act is merely the latest in a long line of legislative and legal battles in the abortion wars. Bitter wrangling over *Roe v. Wade* and subsequent abortion cases stretches back now fifty years. Conservative legal scholars consider *Roe* to be wrongly decided and perhaps the prime example of judicial activism in American history. Even many liberal experts who support abortion rights admit that the legal reasoning behind *Roe* lacks substance.

The basis of the Supreme Court's ruling in *Roe* rests on the individual's right to privacy. This right was first recognized in the 1965 case *Griswold v. Connecticut,* which legalized the purchase of contraceptives by married couples. In his majority opinion in *Griswold,* Justice William O. Douglas could not point to a specific mention of a right to privacy in the Constitution. Instead, he claimed to discover such a right in a *penumbra* (or shadow) formed by *emanations* (or barely perceptible outgrowths) from the Bill of Rights. Two other justices agreed with Douglas, though they cited the due process clause of the Fourteenth Amendment as the grounds to protect personal liberty from government intrusion.

Despite the controversy over its legal reasoning, *Roe,* as a milestone for women's rights, continues to be fiercely defended by its supporters. "The very essence of a constitutional right is that it is not up to the legislatures," says Julie Rikelma, a lawyer for the Center for Reproductive Rights. "It's a right that we all have [that] the legislators cannot take away from us."[19]

However, recent changes to the Supreme Court's makeup have raised concerns that *Roe* and subsequent decisions that affirmed abortion rights are in danger of

"The very essence of a constitutional right is that it is not up to the legislatures. It's a right that we all have [that] the legislators cannot take away from us."[19]

—Julie Rikelma, a lawyer for the Center for Reproductive Rights

Supreme Court justices had no illusions that their 1973 finding of a constitutional right to abortion would steer clear of controversy. *Roe v. Wade* touched on subjects about which most Americans have strong opinions, including when life begins, the moral question of terminating a pregnancy, and how to protect women's rights. The court's decision relied on a previously recognized right to privacy that was not spelled out in the Constitution. With all this in mind, Justice Harry Blackmun, in his majority opinion, conceded that the *Roe* decision was likely to prove polarizing:

> We forthwith acknowledge our awareness of the sensitive and emotional nature of the abortion controversy, of the vigorous opposing views, even among physicians, and of the deep and seemingly absolute convictions that the subject inspires. One's philosophy, one's experiences, one's exposure to the raw edges of human existence, one's religious training, one's attitudes toward life and family and their values, and the moral standards one establishes and seeks to observe, are all likely to influence and to color one's thinking and conclusions about abortion.

Quoted in *Landmark Cases*, "Roe v. Wade: Mr. Justice Blackmun Delivered the Opinion of the Court," C-Span. https://landmarkcases.c-span.org.

being reversed. The court's current six-to-three conservative majority seems willing to revisit the abortion issue. On November 1, 2021, the court declined to block the Heartbeat Act, with Chief Justice John Roberts joining the three liberal justices in dissent. The Texas law instantly became the most restrictive in the nation. The first week that the law went into effect, abortion clinics throughout Texas saw a large drop in scheduled visits. The Supreme Court agreed to hear a more direct challenge to *Roe* in December 2021, and advocates on both sides of the issue are preparing for a historic battle that could change the fate of abortion protections.

Finding a Legal Path Forward

The case that became *Roe v. Wade* also concerned a Texas abortion statute. In 1971 a Dallas waitress named Norma McCorvey consulted a lawyer about ending her pregnancy of twenty weeks. Unable to recommend an abortion, which was illegal under Texas law, her attorney decided to challenge the ban in court. When the case was filed, McCorvey was given the name Jane Roe to shield her identity. Henry Wade, the district attorney of Dallas County, served as stand-in for the state. Those names would become synonymous with the abortion issue in America.

On appeal, *Roe v. Wade* reached the Supreme Court in a matter of months. Following oral arguments in December 1971, seven of the justices leaned toward declaring the Texas abortion law unconstitutional as a violation of privacy rights. Harry Blackmun, a lifelong Republican appointed by Richard Nixon, drew the task of writing the majority opinion. Joined by six other justices, Blackmun cited the *Griswold* decision and asserted that a woman's right to privacy under the Fourteenth Amendment protected her from the scrutiny of the state. Although the majority opinion dismissed the argument that life begins at conception, Blackmun was also faced with explaining when the Fourteenth Amendment's guarantees of respecting the fetus's right to life would supersede the mother's right to privacy.

A doctor and patient discuss the results of a fetal ultrasound. States such as Texas have passed laws severely restricting abortions. These states hope that legal challenges will lead to the Supreme Court overturning the 1973 ruling that legalized abortion.

Help arrived in the form of a lower court ruling on an abortion case in Connecticut. District judge Jon O. Newman had ruled that the state ban on abortion could take effect only after the point of viability. Viability, as Newman explained, is the point about halfway between conception and birth when the fetus is capable of surviving, with medical assistance, outside the uterus. In several cases since 1946, viability had been used to protect the rights of the unborn in cases of prenatal injury. For example, in *Bonbrest v. Kotz* (1946), a federal district court allowed a viable infant plaintiff to seek damages for injuries suffered during removal from the mother's womb. Nonetheless, Newman was the first judge to include viability as part of a constitutional right to abortion.

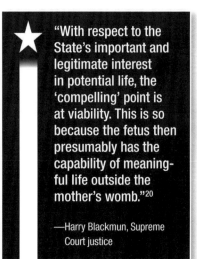

"With respect to the State's important and legitimate interest in potential life, the 'compelling' point is at viability. This is so because the fetus then presumably has the capability of meaningful life outside the mother's womb."[20]

—Harry Blackmun, Supreme Court justice

Justice Lewis F. Powell Jr. quoted Newman's ruling in a letter to Blackmun. The letter convinced Blackmun that he had found a legal path forward. On January 22, 1973, the Supreme Court made abortion a constitutional right up to the point of viability. States could prohibit abortion only in the third trimester of pregnancy, when its interest in protecting potential life outweighed a woman's right to choose. "With respect to the State's important and legitimate interest in potential life," Blackmun explained in his opinion, "the 'compelling' point is at viability. This is so because the fetus then presumably has the capability of meaningful life outside the mother's womb."[20] The court's seven-to-two decision swept aside abortion bans in forty-six states and the District of Columbia. All at once, the United States had one of the most liberal abortion policies in the world.

A Victory, but No End to the Conflict

Feminists hailed the decision as a major victory, not only for women's rights but for women's health. Before *Roe*, women seeking abortions had to get them illegally, which meant they often were performed in conditions that were unsafe and potentially deadly. Legalized abortion promised to be not only safe but also widely available. The procedure could now be performed at licensed clinics staffed by medical professionals. Women could terminate pregnancies caused by rape or incest. Economists predicted that more women would enter the workforce and choose to wait before starting a family.

However, it was clear that the court's decision would not end the controversy. Conservatives attacked *Roe* as a reckless example of judicial activism. They insisted that the life-and-death stakes of abortion called for resolution by state legislatures, and thus by the people, and not by unelected justices. Some accused Blackmun of perpetuating the so-called right to privacy that appeared nowhere in the Constitution. In his dissent, Chief Justice William Rehnquist pointed out that public opinion on abortion seemed certain to remain divided. "Even today, when society's views on abortion are changing," wrote Rehnquist, "the very existence of the debate is evidence that the 'right' to an abortion is not so universally accepted as the appellant would have us believe."[21]

The *Roe* decision led to more passionate disagreements on abortion than ever before. Views on abortion became a litmus test for both liberals and conservatives, crowding out debate on other issues. Supreme Court nominees were routinely grilled on their abortion stance to predict how they might rule in a future challenge to *Roe*.

Subsequent cases only added to the uncertainty. In 1989, a bitterly divided court ruled in *Webster v. Reproductive Health Services* that states could restrict the right to abortion in certain ways, even in the first trimester of pregnancy. The *Webster* ruling upheld a Missouri law that denied state funding for abortion and prohibited state employees from performing or counseling for abortion. The court also declined to overrule the Missouri law's opening statement that life begins at conception. Moreover, four of the justices in the five-to-four majority urged the court to reconsider *Roe*, which outraged Justice Blackmun. In his dissent, he declared, "For today, at least, the law of abortion stands undisturbed. For today, the women of this nation still retain the liberty to control their destinies. But the signs are evident and very ominous, and a chill wind blows."[22]

Three years later, in *Planned Parenthood v. Casey,* the court shifted course again. This time a five-to-four majority upheld *Roe*'s legalization of abortion up to viability. Yet the court also seemed to suggest that the reasoning in *Roe* was faulty because the court scrapped much of *Roe*'s basic framework. Instead, the court introduced a new idea: laws on abortion could not present an undue burden to women seeking the procedure. The ruling provided no clear definition of an undue burden, other than "a substantial obstacle in the path of a woman seeking an abortion before the fetus attains viability."[23] Critics of *Planned Parenthood v. Casey* claimed it was a clumsy attempt at stare decisis that still left the abortion question unsettled. Once again, the Supreme Court stood

Pro-choice and pro-life protesters rally outside the Supreme Court. In the decades since the court ruled in Roe v. Wade, *the abortion debate in the United States has lost none of its intensity.*

accused of judicial activism and making laws from the bench. But liberals praised the ruling as judicial restraint because it reaffirmed the core precedent of *Roe,* which found a constitutional right to abortion under the Fourteenth Amendment.

Science and a New Challenge to Roe

In the three decades since *Casey*, the abortion debate has lost none of its intensity in America. Pro-choice and pro-life groups regularly march on Washington, DC, to display solidarity for their cause. Meanwhile, science has played a growing role in the controversy. Medical experts have long predicted that advances in neonatal care, enabling fetuses to survive outside the uterus earlier in pregnancy, would erode *Roe*'s viability argument. Advances have moved back the viability line from twenty-eight weeks in 1973 to twenty-one weeks today. Thus, with innovative care, it is possible for a developing fetus to survive outside the mother's womb a full month and a half earlier than during the 1970s. However, the technology that has probably altered the debate most is ultrasound imaging. Smartphones across the country contain shared ultrasound images of a fetus in utero, with fingers, toes, and even fingernails visible as early as twelve to thirteen weeks. These pictures counter the argument that before viability outside the womb, the fetus is merely a random clump of cells.

Legal experts believe that the Supreme Court's current six-to-three conservative majority presents the greatest challenge to *Roe* in years. On December 1, 2021, the court heard arguments in *Dobbs v. Jackson Women's Health Organization*. The case involved a Mississippi law that prohibits abortion after fifteen weeks except in medical emergencies or for severe fetal problems. The fifteen-week limit flies in the face of *Roe*'s emphasis on viability for regulating abortions. Like the Texas Heartbeat Act, the Mississippi statute seems clearly unconstitutional according to precedent. Yet pro-choice advocates fear it provides the court with its best opportunity to overturn *Roe*.

During the hearing on *Dobbs,* the court's newest justices, Brett Kavanaugh and Amy Coney Barrett, indicated they were open not

If *Roe v. Wade* Were Overturned

Pro-choice activists warn of dire consequences if *Roe v. Wade* were to be overturned. But should that happen, abortion would not become illegal overnight in the United States. Instead, the question would revert to state legislatures across the nation. Legislators, and ultimately voters, would decide on abortion regulations in each state. Democrat-controlled statehouses would no doubt preserve their abortion laws, whereas Republican-controlled legislatures would either establish tighter controls on the procedure or ban it.

Many states already have passed so-called trigger laws that would immediately take effect should *Roe* be reversed. According to the Guttmacher Institute, a group that tracks reproductive rights, twenty-one states would ban or heavily restrict access to abortion. In fourteen states and the District of Columbia, abortion rights would continue to have explicit protection.

Most worrisome to supporters of abortion are the inevitable curbs on access to the procedure. Experts say 41 percent of females of childbearing age would see their nearest abortion clinic shut down. Most would have to travel hundreds of miles to find an alternative. "A post-Roe United States isn't one in which abortion isn't legal at all," says Caitlin Knowles Myers, an economist at Middlebury College. "It's one in which there's tremendous inequality in abortion access."

Quoted in Quoctrung Bui, Claire Cain Miller, and Margot Sanger-Katz, "Where Abortion Access Would Decline If Roe v. Wade Were Overturned," *New York Times,* May 18, 2021. www.nytimes.com.

only to affirming the Mississippi law but also to overruling *Roe* as a mistaken decision. Chief Justice Roberts, who has striven to protect the court's public image and authority, seemed likely to pursue a compromise that would keep some form of abortion rights in place. The three liberal justices tried to stress the importance of standing by major precedents such as *Roe*. But they also seemed reconciled to protesting in dissent. Stephen Breyer warned the court about the dangers of buckling to political pressure. Sonia Sotomayor was even more pointed in her remarks to her colleagues: "Will this institution survive the stench that this creates in the public perception that the Constitution and its reading are just political acts? I don't see how it is possible."[24] But Sotomayor's comments will not likely stave off further courtroom challenges to what many acknowledge has always been a controversial Supreme Court decision. The rulings in these challenge cases may indicate the future of *Roe v. Wade*.

CHAPTER FOUR

The Battle over Voting Rights

On March 3, 2021, the House passed the For the People Act, which aimed to protect voting rights in the states. The bill included measures to expand early voting and vote-by-mail procedures, modernize voting systems, restore voting rights for former prison inmates, and mandate automatic voter registration. According to House Democrats, these voter protections would apply across the nation to prevent state legislatures from suppressing the vote.

Passage of the bill came after a contentious year that saw changes in voting procedures due to the COVID-19 pandemic, false claims of voter fraud from presidential candidate Donald Trump, what Democrats saw as restrictive voting laws passed in response to those unsubstantiated claims, and growing calls among Democrats to safeguard voting rights. The For the People Act passed by a narrow margin of 220 votes in favor and 210 against, with only one Republican joining the Democratic majority. "The right to vote is sacred and fundamental—it is the right from which all of our rights as Americans springs," said President Joe Biden in praising the bill. "This landmark legislation is urgently needed to protect that right, to safeguard the integrity of our elections, and to repair and strengthen our democracy."[25]

The bill had almost no chance of passage in the Senate, where Democrats lacked the necessary votes. Yet even had the Senate rubber-stamped the bill, it likely would have faced a strong legal challenge, all the way to the Supreme Court. According to the Constitution, the states are responsible for elections, even national presidential elections. States have traditionally been free to conduct their elections as they see fit, as long as all eligible voters have equal access to the ballot. Yet Republicans in Congress considered the For the People Act a blatant attempt to federalize elections in the United States. Whether the conservative majority on the Supreme Court would agree and forbid such a move was a question for the future. But if so, it would only continue the court's history of judicial activism on voting rights in America.

Creating the Standard of One Person, One Vote

In 1962 the Supreme Court decided the first major case to address voting rights in the United States. Previously, complaints about how legislative districts were drawn had been left to Congress and the states. The 1946 case *Colegrove v. Green* had made the point explicit. "The short of it is that the Constitution has conferred upon Congress exclusive authority to secure fair representation by the States in the popular House," wrote Justice Felix Frankfurter. "If Congress failed in exercising its powers, whereby standards of fairness are offended, the remedy ultimately lies with the people."[26]

This went along with accepted ideas of federalism, which is the constitutional principle that grants specific powers to the federal government and reserves all other powers to the states or the people.

Under the US federalist system, political disputes are decided in the states. In 1961, however, Charles Baker and a group of Tennessee citizens brought a suit claiming that their voting rights had been violated by state lawmakers. Baker noted that the state of Tennessee had

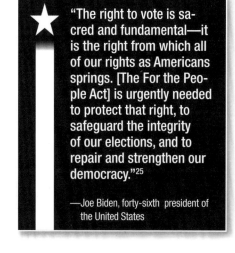

"The right to vote is sacred and fundamental—it is the right from which all of our rights as Americans springs. [The For the People Act] is urgently needed to protect that right, to safeguard the integrity of our elections, and to repair and strengthen our democracy."[25]

—Joe Biden, forty-sixth president of the United States

not redrawn its map of legislative districts since 1901, a period of sixty years. During that time, the state's population had shifted significantly to urban areas. Yet the old district map gave sparsely populated districts the same political clout as more densely populated ones. According to Baker's suit, this was unconstitutional under the equal protection clause of the Fourteenth Amendment. However, the US District Court in Tennessee dismissed the complaint. The district court said it lacked authority to intervene in such a political matter under the *Colegrove* ruling.

When *Baker v. Carr* reached the Supreme Court under appeal, legal analysts expected a quick affirmation of the *Colegrove* precedent. But a majority of the justices saw a larger principle at stake. Voting rights could be diluted through unfairly drawn districts, giving some votes more weight than others. Some of the justices agonized over the decision, fearing it was an assault on the federalist framework of the Constitution. The strain of the case caused one justice, Charles Evans Whittaker, to remove himself for health reasons.

Finally, by a six-to-two majority led by liberal justice William Brennan, the court decided that the case was properly within its jurisdiction. The court ruled in Baker's favor, opening the door to changes in the Tennessee map of legislative districts.

Frankfurter, who had urged the court to stay out of political disputes in *Colegrove,* penned a blistering dissent in *Baker*. He considered the *Baker* ruling an outrageous example of judicial activism—or, in his words, "destructively novel judicial power"[27]— and worried that it would erode public confidence in the court. But the case set a new standard in which the Supreme Court could intervene to protect voting rights.

In subsequent cases, such as *Reynolds v. Sims* (1964), the court declared that voting districts across states had to be roughly equal in population. That meant that districts should be drawn according to the number of people within the boundaries, not by equivalent geographic size. As Chief Justice Earl Warren stated in *Reynolds,* "Legislators represent people, not acres or trees. Legislators are elected by voters, not farms or cities or

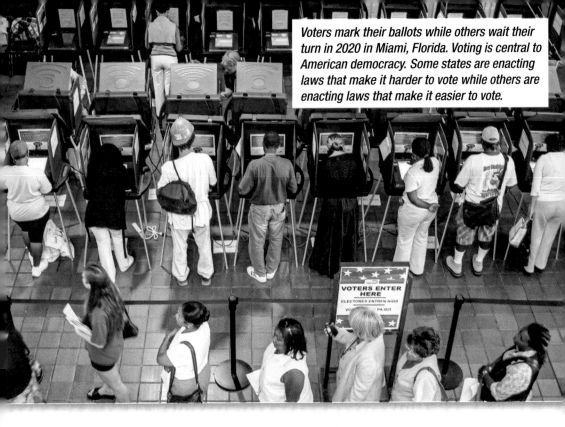

Voters mark their ballots while others wait their turn in 2020 in Miami, Florida. Voting is central to American democracy. Some states are enacting laws that make it harder to vote while others are enacting laws that make it easier to vote.

economic interests."[28] This created the formula of one person, one vote, in which each vote must weigh the same under the equal protection clause. Over the next few years, *Reynolds* and similar lawsuits led to state legislatures across the country redrawing unequal district maps.

Addressing the Problem of Gerrymandering

The Supreme Court also has addressed a related area of voting rights: gerrymandering. This is when state legislatures redraw voting districts purely for partisan advantage. The court took up the issue of gerrymandering in 1993 with *Shaw v. Reno*. The case involved North Carolina's newly drawn congressional district map based on population changes in the 1990 census. The US Department of Justice rejected the state's district plan because it contained only one so-called majority-minority district. Such a district has more minority voters—in this case, Black voters— than White voters. Attorney General Janet Reno directed North

Carolina's state assembly to add a second majority-minority district to comply with recent changes to the Voting Rights Act (VRA) designed to bolster minority voting strength.

As drawn by the state assembly, this second district had a bizarre shape. It meandered as a narrow strip, following a highway nearly all the way across the state. A group of White voters in North Carolina, headed by Ruth O. Shaw, challenged the new map. Shaw's group claimed that the map was redrawn strictly to create another Black-majority district. And indeed it was, to counter years of districts having been drawn to benefit White candidates in a state with a large Black population. However, Shaw's group argued that creating districts on a racial basis violated the equal protection clause. Therefore, the new district, with its odd shape, represented an unconstitutional gerrymander.

In a five-to-four decision, the Supreme Court agreed with Shaw that the district's odd shape could not be explained except

The Origin of the Gerrymander

A common practice that influences voting rights in America is gerrymandering. State commissions sometimes employ tremendous ingenuity in redrawing legislative districts to gain partisan advantage. Boundary lines can extend for miles along rivers, make sudden detours into adjacent districts, or balloon into certain neighborhoods to include voters of a certain party, color, or ethnicity. Political opponents often complain about the unfairness and the assault on voting integrity—until they do the same thing themselves the next time.

The term *gerrymander* comes from a political cartoon that appeared in the *Boston Gazette* in 1812. The cartoon described a new species of monster, shaped like a salamander, that it called "the Gerry-mander." The "monster" was a bizarrely shaped voting district in the Boston area, named for the state's governor, Elbridge Gerry. By approving the unusual boundary for his party's benefit, Gerry, one of the nation's founders, was forever saddled with the namesake in American politics. As historian Erick Trickey notes, "It has overshadowed all of Gerry's other accomplishments in history." Today, despite Supreme Court rulings to limit the practice, the monster Gerry-mander still lurks in the political shadows.

Erick Trickey, "Where Did the Term 'Gerrymander' Come From?," *Smithsonian Magazine*, July 20, 2017. www.smithsonian.com.

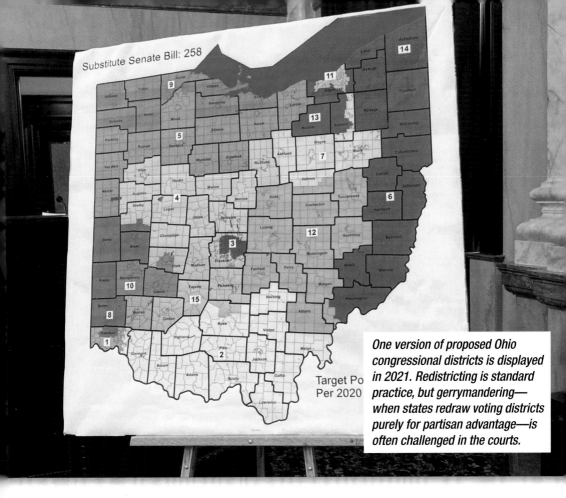

Substitute Senate Bill: 258

One version of proposed Ohio congressional districts is displayed in 2021. Redistricting is standard practice, but gerrymandering—when states redraw voting districts purely for partisan advantage—is often challenged in the courts.

as a way to separate voters by race. And it declared that although race could be taken into consideration in drawing district lines, it could not be the main purpose. But the court also held that laws that introduce a classification by race have to meet a standard of strict scrutiny. This means they must have a compelling government purpose, be narrowly focused to accomplish that goal, and be the least restrictive way to accomplish it. Ultimately, the court found that North Carolina's redrawn district map did not satisfy the standard of strict scrutiny.

Critics sounded the alarm about the court's unwillingness to support the VRA's racial objectives. In essence, they rejected the court's use of judicial restraint. Without redrawn districts, they said, minority candidates had no greater chance of being elected. "In the aftermath of the [Shaw] ruling, civil rights activists were left in a bind," says Christian Hosam, a researcher on political reform at the liberal think tank New America. "The VRA itself mandated that states needed to address their underrepresentation of minority influence, but now the court was saying that using race as a singular factor was unconstitutional."[29]

A Dispute over Racial Progress and Voting Rights

A redistricting plan also played a part in 2013's *Shelby v. Holder,* a voting rights case that continues to draw ferocious criticism from the political left. The redistricting plan came from Shelby County, Alabama, which was challenging part of the 1965 VRA. In passing the VRA, Congress had found that race-based voting discrimination, including such practices as gerrymandering, occurred much more often in certain regions of the country. According to Section 5 of the VRA, states in these areas could not make changes to their voting laws or practices without first getting them cleared by the US attorney general or US District Court. This oversight, called preclearance, involved assuring that the change would not deny or abridge anyone's right to vote by race or color.

Shelby County challenged Section 5 as being unconstitutional. It claimed that the rule was based on old data, its coverage formula was outdated, and conditions regarding race and voting rights in Shelby County had improved considerably since 1965. Shelby County insisted it should be able to carry out its redistricting plan without a federal review.

To the outrage of liberals and many media outlets, the Roberts court upheld Shelby County's challenge by a vote of five to four. In his majority opinion, Roberts essentially said that Shelby County had made substantial racial progress since 1965. While admitting that voter discrimination still exists, he suggested that the VRA's formula for treating certain states differently regarding race was no longer based on current conditions. "There is no denying . . . that the conditions that originally justified these measures no longer characterize voting in the covered jurisdictions," said Roberts. "Nearly 50 years later, things have changed dramatically."[30]

The liberal justices slammed the conservative majority for, in their view, gutting a vital part of the VRA. Justice Ginsburg, a longtime champion of civil rights, delivered a stinging dissent. She agreed that voting discrimination had decreased overall yet stressed that the improvement was due to the ongoing influence of the VRA. As Ginsburg said, "Throwing out preclearance when it has worked and is continuing to work to stop discriminatory changes is like throwing away your umbrella in a rainstorm because you are not getting wet."[31]

> "Throwing out preclearance [in the VRA] when it has worked and is continuing to work to stop discriminatory changes is like throwing away your umbrella in a rainstorm because you are not getting wet."[31]
>
> —Ruth Bader Ginsburg, Supreme Court justice

Justice Ruth Bader Ginsburg (shown in an official Supreme Court portrait) strenuously objected to the majority ruling allowing states with a history of race-based voting discrimination to change their voting laws without federal oversight.

Setting Further Limits on the VRA

Liberal critics claimed that the ruling in *Shelby* represented obvious judicial activism on the conservative side. They blasted the majority justices for blunting a congressional law that had protected minority voting rights for decades. They pointed out that *Shelby* did not just affect one county in Alabama; instead, it released nine states from preclearance oversight. They also warned that it would bring a flood of new voting restrictions in states that no longer had to fear oversight under the VRA. And in fact, several states did immediately pass restrictions, such as voter identification requirements and bans on election day registration. Lower courts have accused lawmakers in certain states of targeting minority voters with almost surgical precision. Civil rights activists contend that Republican-controlled legislatures remain determined to suppress the Black vote. They fear that the problem could grow worse when a new round of redistricting begins based on the 2020 census. "Since *Shelby,* states have really opened the floodgates to voter suppression," says Leigh Chapman, director of the voting rights program at the Leadership Conference on Civil and Human Rights, "and we've seen laws that have discriminated against voters of color all across the country."[32]

"Since *Shelby*, states have really opened the floodgates to voter suppression, and we've seen laws that have discriminated against voters of color all across the country."[32]

—Leigh Chapman, director of the voting rights program at the Leadership Conference on Civil and Human Rights

On July 1, 2021, the Supreme Court dealt a further blow to the VRA by upholding two Arizona laws. One forbade the collection of absentee ballots by anyone other than a relative or caregiver. The other disallowed ballots cast in the wrong precinct. The court's ruling addressed procedures covered in Section 2 of the VRA, which prohibits voting practices that deny citizens equal access to the ballot on account of race, color, or membership in a minority language group. In her dissent, Justice Elena Kagan pointed once more

A Closer Look at Ballot Harvesting

One of the issues in the Arizona voting rights case, *Brnovich v. Democratic National Committee,* was ballot collection—or what opponents call "ballot harvesting." The court affirmed the state's law forbidding the collection of a voter's absentee ballot by anyone other than a postal worker, an election official, or the voter's family member, caregiver, or household member. During the COVID-affected election of November 2020, procedures such as mail-in voting and ballot collection were commonly used for voters' safety and convenience. Certain states, such as Arizona and its Republican-controlled legislature, have moved to prevent such practices from becoming a permanent addition.

Some legal experts see the value of collecting ballots but also recognize possible abuses. As Richard L. Hasen, professor of law and political science at the University of California, Irvine, explains, "Allowing collection in certain circumstances makes sense, such as for voters in remote locations, or elderly or disabled voters who might have trouble returning their own ballots. But . . . such collection may provide the pathway for unscrupulous people to destroy or alter ballots."

Quoted in Nancy Martorano Miller et al., "Is Ballot Collection, or 'Ballot Harvesting,' Good for Democracy? We Asked 5 Experts," The Conversation, March 15, 2021. https://theconversation.com.

to judicial activism that usurps powers belonging to Congress. Kagan claimed that the court's ruling had blunted the VRA's protections for minority voting rights. "This Court has no right to remake Section 2," wrote Kagan. "Maybe some think that vote suppression is a relic of history—and so the need for a potent Section 2 has come and gone. . . . But Congress gets to make that call."[33]

Conservatives generally agree with the court's latest rulings on voting rights, viewing them as a corrective to previous activist decisions. They point out that laws to protect ballot integrity like those in Arizona did not negatively affect voter turnout in the 2020 election, which broke all records. They also contend that Republican-controlled legislatures have retained many COVID-era measures for early voting and vote-by-mail for voters' convenience (claims that many liberal and nonpartisan groups dispute). However, conservatives also stress that elections must have rules and safeguards to protect public confidence in the vote. Such stark disagreements over the issue of voting rights promises to draw even more scrutiny of future Supreme Court rulings.

CHAPTER FIVE

Maintaining the Court's Integrity

In early December 2021, President Biden's thirty-four-member Presidential Commission on the Supreme Court released its eagerly anticipated report. The commission took seven months to study possible reforms to the court. It held six public meetings and received input from forty-four expert witnesses. In the end, the report did not recommend structural changes to the court, as some progressives had hoped. Instead, the bipartisan panel laid out arguments for and against reforms such as adding justices to the court, setting term limits for justices, and limiting the court's jurisdiction in certain ways. With regard to Congress reshaping the court, the report noted the many uncertainties involved, including loss of public trust. "The court would have to decide on the constitutionality of a law that restructures the court itself. There might also be strong disagreements about which justices should participate in the decision," the report states. "No matter which way the court came out on the question, these commissioners worry that the court's legitimacy, or perceptions of its legitimacy, would be undermined."[34]

Falling Approval Ratings

The commission's report arrived amid falling approval rates for the Supreme Court. A Gallup poll in late September 2021 showed the American public's approval of the court diving to below 40 percent from 49 percent in July. This rating was the court's lowest since 2000. Thirty-seven percent of those polled thought the Supreme Court had become too conservative. Pollsters linked the public's dissatisfaction to the court's late-summer emergency rulings against two key Biden administration policies on evictions and immigration. Plus, there was growing bitterness at the court's refusal to block the Texas Heartbeat Act, which banned nearly all abortions beyond six weeks of pregnancy. And with an upcoming docket filled with divisive cases on abortion, voting rights, and firearm regulations, the court almost certainly faces more controversy ahead.

Observers on the left and right have expressed concern about these trends. Liberals accuse the conservative justices on the court with politicizing its decisions. Too often, they say, the right-leaning justices rule according to their political preferences, leading the public to see the court itself as too political. Even Lisa Murkowski, a Republican senator from Alaska, sees potential risks. "I worry a great deal about it, because when the public begins to question and doubt the independence of this third, separate but equal branch of government, they've got a problem here," she says. "I think the public needs to be able to trust that the judiciary will be that independent, unbiased check [on the other two branches]."[35]

Chief Justice Roberts has long been outspoken in defending the federal judiciary from charges of political bias. In November 2018, when President Trump referred to an adverse ruling as coming from an "Obama judge," Roberts was quick to object: "We do not have Obama judges or Trump judges, Bush judges or Clinton judges. What we have is an extraordinary group of dedicated judges doing their level best to do equal right to those appearing before them. That independent judiciary is something we

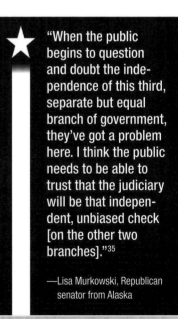

"When the public begins to question and doubt the independence of this third, separate but equal branch of government, they've got a problem here. I think the public needs to be able to trust that the judiciary will be that independent, unbiased check [on the other two branches]."[35]

—Lisa Murkowski, Republican senator from Alaska

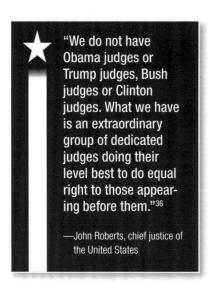

should all be thankful for."[36] Reports suggest, however, that Roberts fears a growing public perception that the current Supreme Court is swayed by politics. Court observers believe this concern may lead Roberts to try to fashion compromise rulings on abortion and voting rights.

Even the court's newest justice, Barrett, has responded publicly to accusations of a biased court. In a September 2021 speech, she told a Kentucky audience, "My goal today is to convince you that this court is not comprised of a bunch of partisan hacks."[37] Critics pointed out that she was speaking at an event for Senator McConnell, the architect of the court's current conservative majority.

Right-wing pundits mostly dismiss the accusations of bias. They say that the court's opponents mistake conservative judicial philosophy for partisanship. They also suggest that public disap-

A Gallup poll in late September 2021 showed the American public's approval of the Supreme Court diving to below 40 percent from 49 percent in July. This rating was the court's lowest since 2000.

proval of rulings on contentious issues is something that every Supreme Court in American history has endured. And charges of partisanship are nothing new. Under President Obama, for example, a Gallup survey found that 37 percent of Americans considered the Supreme Court too liberal.

Countering the Court's Shift to the Right

Frustrated by what they see as the current Supreme Court's increasing judicial activism, progressives are pushing for changes to counter the court's shift to the right. That is why President Biden created, by executive order, his presidential commission. Although opponents on the right did not see the need for the commission, and criticized it as politically motivated, its members represented a mix of political viewpoints. It was divided roughly into three groups: conservatives, moderate liberals, and progressives. The conservatives rejected any major changes to the court as potentially disastrous. The moderate liberals—the largest group—fretted about attacks on democracy in America but also felt that remaking the court at such a polarized time would only weaken its standing among the public. And the small but vocal group of progressives felt the court had already lost its legitimacy and desperately needed reform.

One of the main proposals that the commission explored was adding justices to the Supreme Court to change its political balance. For years the court has been narrowly divided on landmark cases involving such topics as health care, gun rights, and same-sex marriage. A single swing vote, often cast by now-retired justice Anthony Kennedy, proved decisive in several controversial five-to-four decisions. The moderate Kennedy sometimes sided with the court's liberals, sometimes with the conservatives. Today, with conservatives owning a six-to-three advantage, many observers fear a spate of activist rulings that would lurch the nation to the political right. But others are not so sure. "We'll just have to see what happens," says Lee Epstein, a political scientist at Washington University in St. Louis. "When the center of the court

Court-Packing at the State Level

Conservatives have blasted court-packing as a radical move that would politicize the Supreme Court. Yet a study published early in 2020 shows that court-packing schemes, by both parties, are hardly unknown at the state level. In recent years, eleven states have attempted to reshape their courts for partisan advantage. And the two states where the moves succeeded have Republican-controlled legislatures.

Marin Levy, a law professor at Duke University and author of the study, says court-packing at the state level is growing more frequent. In Arizona, for example, Republicans passed a bill in 2016 expanding the number of state supreme court justices from five to seven. Arizona's Republican governor was able to appoint the two new justices shortly after passage. Also in 2016, Republicans in Georgia added two justices to that state's supreme court, bringing the total to nine. The initiative sought rulings that favored business interests in Georgia.

Levy's study shows support for court-packing, at least at the state level. "If court packing and unpacking were considered strictly [forbidden]," says Levy, "one would not expect to see over twenty different bills to pack and unpack the highest court in eleven different states."

Quoted in Christopher Ingraham, "GOP Has Been Aggressively Trying to Pack Supreme Courts at State Level, Study Says," *Washington Post,* October 13, 2020. www.washingtonpost.com.

moves right, will the justices feel like, 'You know what, there's nothing stopping us, we're going to plow ahead'? That might very well happen. But they might also get a little cautious."[38]

Progressives and some liberals have urged Biden to shift the court's balance by adding four left-leaning justices, giving the left control of a thirteen-member panel. Such an initiative, called court-packing, was first contemplated back in the 1930s. In 1937, Democratic president Franklin D. Roosevelt threatened the maneuver when conservatives on the court continued to block his New Deal legislation during the Great Depression. Roosevelt finally withdrew his plan in the face of strong public opposition. Since then, court-packing has been viewed as too radical a step for serious consideration.

Nonetheless, the idea has supporters. Activist groups such as Take Back the Court and Demand Justice say the current situation in Washington, DC, is a crisis that calls for radical measures. Like many on the left, they believe Trump and Republicans broke faith with America by filling Justice Ginsburg's seat one month before the 2020 election after blocking Obama's nomination in 2016. The excuse given at the time was that it was too close to the next presidential election, which was eight months away. Fairness, they say, warrants rebalancing the court along political lines. In place of the term *court-packing*, however, activists prefer the more neutral *court expansion.* And they justify the move historically. "The size of the court has changed six times in American history," says Aaron Belkin, the director of Take Back the Court, "and the Constitution clearly gives Congress the right to shape the contours of the court."[39]

Chief Justice John Roberts (shown in an official Supreme Court portrait) has long been outspoken in defending the federal judiciary from charges of political bias.

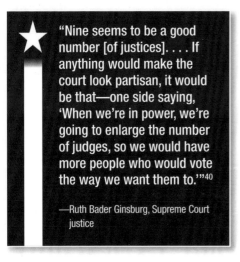
But in interviews, Ginsburg herself firmly rejected the notion. "Nine seems to be a good number [of justices]. It's been that way for a long time," she told National Public Radio in 2019. "If anything would make the court look partisan, it would be that—one side saying, 'When we're in power, we're going to enlarge the number of judges, so we would have more people who would vote the way we want them to.'"[40] President Biden has also admitted that he is not in favor of expanding the court.

Limiting the Terms of Justices

Biden's presidential commission also debated other suggestions for change. One idea is to limit the terms of justices. Currently, each justice serves a lifetime term, subject only to removal by impeachment for some form of bad behavior. However, a growing number of legal experts from both parties are open to the idea of term limits. They say that it would help avoid situations in which a justice is slowed by age or poor health and is less able to perform the job with vigor and mental sharpness. Moreover, setting term limits would ensure more frequent turnover on the court. Terms could be staggered by two years to allow for regular appointments. Instituting term limits would likely call for a constitutional amendment, although some scholars believe Congress could work around this requirement.

On September 29, 2020, California Democrat Ro Khanna introduced a term limits bill in the House. The bill would establish eighteen-year terms for Supreme Court justices and also limit the Senate's advice and consent authority in the court's appointment process. If the Senate neglected to act on a nomination within 120 days—as happened with Obama's

Stripping the Supreme Court's Jurisdiction

Among the more radical proposals to rein in the Supreme Court is to limit its jurisdiction. That means stripping away its authority to hear certain kinds of cases. Proponents point out that Article III, Section 2 of the Constitution allows Congress to make exceptions to the Supreme Court's ability to hear cases on appeal. For example, to protect legislation on campaign finance reform from being overturned by the court, Congress could strip away its judicial review function on this topic. Disputes could ultimately be decided by voters, who could replace legislators if they disagree with the maneuver.

To counter Trump's appointments of conservative judges all the way up to the Supreme Court, some progressive legal scholars prefer a radical approach. "The better option is to shrink the role of courts and stop permitting them to determine winners and losers in so many of our political disputes," says Christopher J. Sprigman, codirector of New York University's Engelberg Center on Innovation Law and Policy. "Reining in the role of courts is the best way to kill the incentive that drives both parties to appoint activists to the federal bench." Time will tell if the American people will support such extreme measures going forward.

Christopher J. Sprigman, "A Constitutional Weapon for Biden to Vanquish Trump's Army of Judges," *New Republic,* August 20, 2020. www.newrepublic.com.

nomination of Merrick Garland—the Senate's ability to block the nominee would be waived. The bill also would stagger the terms of sitting justices, create a new level of semiretired senior justices, and require the president to appoint a new justice every two years. In promoting his bill, Khanna said, "No justice should feel the weight of an entire country on their shoulders. No president should be able to shift the ideology of our highest judicial body by mere chance. . . . It's time to standardize and democratize the Supreme Court."[41] Although Khanna's bill has sparked debate on the issue, its passage by the full Congress remains unlikely.

Opponents of Khanna's bill contend that term limits would likely make Supreme Court appointments, and the court itself, more political rather than less. They believe that the security of a lifetime appointment actually helps insulate the justices from political concerns. In making this claim, some refer to the words of

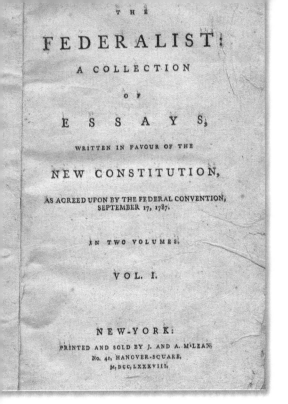

an American founder. "Nothing can contribute so much to [the court's] firmness and independence, as permanency in office," wrote Alexander Hamilton in *The Federalist* in 1788. "This quality may therefore be justly regarded as an indispensable ingredient in its constitution."[42]

An Endless Debate

The debate on how to reform the Supreme Court, or restore its historic balance, seems to have no end in today's polarized political sphere. For now, there is little support for extreme steps such as expanding the court or mandating term limits. Yet there is continuing concern that charges of political bias will weaken the people's trust in the court's rulings.

Sometimes the partisan wars are exaggerated. Legal experts point out that even a politically divided court issues many more unanimous decisions than most people realize. And moderates such as Chief Justice Roberts often seek compromises based on judicial restraint to preserve the court's public standing. As the Supreme Court prepares to rule on a number of divisive cases, Americans of all political views will await the results with hope—and more than a little anxiety.

SOURCE NOTES

Introduction: Restraint in a Time of Polarization

1. Quoted in Melissa Gira Grant, "Amy Coney Barrett's Gentle Deceptions," *New Republic,* October 14, 2020. https://newrepublic.com.
2. Quoted in Nina Totenberg, "Obamacare Wins for the 3rd Time at the Supreme Court," *Morning Edition,* NPR, June 17, 2021. www.npr.org.
3. Ilya Shapiro, "The Impact of Judicial Activism on the Moral Character of Citizens," Cato Institute, October 28, 2010. www.cato.org.

Chapter One: The Supreme Court's Role in a Healthy Democracy

4. Rachel Shelden, "The Supreme Court Used to Be Openly Political. It Traded Partisanship for Power," *Washington Post,* September 25, 2020. www.washingtonpostcom.
5. Quoted in Richard W. Garnett and David A. Strauss, "Article III, Section One," National Constitution Center. https://constitutioncenter.org.
6. Quoted in Legal Information Institute, "William Marbury v. James Madison, Secretary of State of the United States," Cornell Law School. www.law.cornell.edu.
7. Quoted in *Constitution Daily* (blog), "Brown v. Board: When the Supreme Court Ruled Against Segregation," National Constitution Center, May 17, 2021. https://constitutioncenter.org.
8. Quoted in Niskanen Center, "How the Supreme Court Shapes (and Is Shaped by) Its Public Support," podcast, July 15, 2020. www.niskanencenter.org.
9. Ilya Shapiro, "Government Can't Simply Ignore Judicial Rulings It Doesn't Like," Cato Institute, August 13, 2013. www.cato.org.
10. Quoted in Legal Information Institute, "28 U.S. Code # 453–Oaths of Justices and Judges," Cornell Law School. www.law.cornell.edu.
11. Bruce Peabody, "How the Supreme Court Can Maintain Its Legitimacy Amid Intensifying Partisanship," The Conversation, October 20, 2020. https://theconversation.com.

Chapter Two: Activism Versus Restraint over the Years

12. Orin S. Kerr, "Upholding the Law," *Legal Affairs,* March/April 2003. www.legalaffairs.org.

13. Jay Willis, "The Supreme Court's War on Miranda Rights in America," The Appeal, June 23, 2020. https://theappeal.org.
14. Quoted in Keenan D. Kmiec, "The Origin and Current Meanings of 'Judicial Activism,'" *California Law Review,* 2004. https://lawcat.berkeley.edu.
15. Quoted in Prachi Agrawal, "Judicial Activism and Constitutional Challenges in India," *Academike,* November 13, 2014. www.lawoctopus.com.
16. Quoted in Adam J. White, "'Oliver Wendell Holmes' Review: The Maximal Minimalist," *Wall Street Journal,* May 24, 2019. www.wsj.com.
17. Quoted in Brennan Center for Justice, "History." www.brennancenter.org.

Chapter Three: The Abortion Controversy

18. Quoted in Jenna Greene, "Decision Blocking Texas Abortion Law 'Not the Final Word,' Says Bill's Sponsor," Reuters, October 7, 2021. www.reuters.com.
19. Quoted in Nina Totenberg, "Supreme Court Considers Whether to Reverse Roe v. Wade," *Morning Edition,* NPR, December 1, 2021. www.npr.org.
20. Quoted in *Landmark Cases*, "Roe v. Wade: Mr. Justice Blackmun Delivered the Opinion of the Court," C-Span. http://landmarkcases.c-span.org.
21. Quoted in *Landmark Cases*, "Roe v. Wade: Mr. Justice Rehnquist, Dissenting," C-Span. http://landmarkcases.c-span.org.
22. Quoted in Al Kamen, "Supreme Court Restricts Right to Abortion, Giving States Wide Latitude for Regulation," *Washington Post,* July 4, 1989. www.washingtonpost.com.
23. Quoted in Margaret Datiles Watts, "What Constitutes an 'Undue Burden' on a Woman's Right to Abortion?," Culture of Life Foundation, September 24, 2015. https://cultureoflife.org.
24. Quoted in Dareh Gregorian, "Sotomayor Suggests Supreme Court Won't 'Survive the Stench' of Overturning Roe v. Wade," NBC News, December 1, 2021. www.nbcnews.com.

Chapter Four: The Battle over Voting Rights

25. Quoted in Dartunorro Clark, "House Passes Sweeping Voting Rights, Ethics Bill," NBC News, March 4, 2021. www.nbcnews.com.
26. Quoted in Justia: US Supreme Court, "Colegrove v. Green 328 U.S. 549 (1946)." https://supreme.justia.com.
27. Quoted in Jonathan Stahl, "Baker v. Carr: The Supreme Court Gets Involved in Redistricting," *Constitution Daily* (blog), National Constitution Center, December 7, 2015. https://constitutioncenter.org.

28. Quoted in Elianna Spitzer, "Reynolds v. Sims: Supreme Court Case, Arguments, Impact," ThoughtCo, January 10, 2020. www.thoughtco.com.
29. Christian Hosam, "The Supreme Court's Long War Against Voting Rights," *Washington Post,* June 15, 2018. www.washingtonpost.com.
30. Quoted in Joyce White Vance, "Ruth Bader Ginsburg Lost Her Battle to Save Voting Rights. Here's How We Can Take Up the Fight and Honor Her Legacy," *Time,* September 21, 2020. www.time.com.
31. Quoted in Vance, "Ruth Bader Ginsburg Lost Her Battle to Save Voting Rights."
32. Quoted in P.R. Lockhart, "How Shelby County v. Holder Upended Voting Rights in America," Vox, June 25, 2019. www.vox.com.
33. Quoted in Nina Totenberg, "The Supreme Court Deals a New Blow to Voting Rights, Upholding Arizona Restrictions," *Morning Edition,* NPR, July 1, 2021. www.npr.org.

Chapter Five: Maintaining the Court's Integrity

34. Quoted in Melissa Quinn, "Biden's Supreme Court Commission Votes to Submit Report on Reforms," CBS News, December 8, 2021. www.cbsnews.com.
35. Quoted in Robert Barnes and Seung Min Kim, "Supreme Court Observers See Trouble Ahead as Public Approval of Justices Erodes," *Washington Post,* September 26, 2021. www.washingtonpost.com.
36. Quoted in Adam Liptak, "Chief Justice Defends Judicial Independence After Trump Attacks 'Obama Judge,'" *New York Times,* November 21, 2018. www.nytimes.com.
37. Quoted in Barnes and Kim, "Supreme Court Observers See Trouble Ahead as Public Approval of Justices Erodes."
38. Quoted in Amelia Thomson-DeVeaux and Laura Bronner, "How a Conservative 6–3 Majority Would Reshape the Supreme Court," FiveThirtyEight, September 28, 2020. www.fivethirtyeight.com.
39. Quoted in Adam Liptak, "The Precedent, and Perils, of Court Packing," *New York Times,* October 12, 2020. www.nytimes.com.
40. Quoted in Nina Totenberg, "Justice Ginsburg: 'I Am Very Much Alive,'" *Morning Edition,* NPR, July 24, 2019. www.npr.org.
41. Quoted in GovTrack Insider, "Supreme Court Term Limits and Regular Appointments Act Would Establish 18-Year Terms and Nominations Every Two Years," November 9, 2020. https://govtrackinsider.com.
42. Avalon Project, "The Federalist Papers: No. 78," Yale Law School. https://avalon.law.yale.edu.

FOR FURTHER RESEARCH

Books

Carol Anderson, *One Person, No Vote: How Voter Suppression Is Destroying Our Democracy*. New York: Bloomsbury, 2019.

Adam Cohen, *Supreme Inequality: The Supreme Court's Fifty-Year Battle for a More Unjust America*. New York: Penguin, 2020.

Joshua Prager, *The Family Roe: An American Story*. New York: W.W. Norton, 2021.

Mark Tushnet, *Taking Back the Constitution: Activist Judges and the Next Age of American Law*. New Haven, CT: Yale University Press, 2020.

Keith E. Whittington, *Repugnant Laws: Judicial Review of Acts of Congress from the Founding to the Present*. Lawrence: University Press of Kansas, 2019.

Internet Sources

Jess Bravin, "Supreme Court Sends Mixed Signals in Voting Rights Case," *Wall Street Journal,* March 2, 2021. www.wsj.com.

Quoctrung Bui, Claire Cain Miller, and Margot Sanger-Katz, "Where Abortion Access Would Decline If Roe v. Wade Were Overturned," *New York Times,* May 18, 2021. www.nytimes.com.

Daniel Epps and Ganesh Sitaraman, "The Future of Supreme Court Reform," *Harvard Law Review,* May 30, 2021. https://harvardlawreview.org.

Dylan Matthews, "The Supreme Court Is Too Powerful and Anti-Democratic. Here's How We Can Scale Back Its Influence," Vox, September 29, 2020. www.vox.com.

Amber Phillips, "What Is Court Packing, and Why Are Some Democrats Seriously Considering It?," *Washington Post,* October 8, 2020. www.washingtonpost.com.

Websites

Brookings Institution
www.brookings.edu
The Brookings Institution is a nonprofit public policy organization whose mission is to research new ideas for solving problems facing society at the local, national, and global levels. Its website reviews issues related to the Supreme Court and judicial activism.

Constitutional Accountability Center
www.theusconstitution.org
The Constitutional Accountability Center is a think tank dedicated to fulfilling the progressive promise of the US Constitution. It works to preserve the rights and freedoms of Americans and protect the judiciary from politics and special interests. Its website discusses Supreme Court actions related to civil rights, voting rights, and criminal justice.

Hoover Institution
www.hoover.org
The Hoover Institution is a public policy think tank that advances ideas that promote economic opportunity and prosperity while securing and safeguarding peace for America. Its scholars offer policy proposals that seek to address current problems in American society.

Supreme Court of the United States
www.supremecourt.gov
The website for the US Supreme Court features reviews of recent cases and transcripts of the court's proceedings. There is also information about the history of the court and its day-to-day administration.